# the Sacred Feminine

Other Books By James Galluzzo

A Spiritual Handbook: A Resource for Travelers and Guides on the Journey
The Spirituality of Mary Magdalene
Jesus as Liberator and the Gospel Values
Quotes and Reflection Questions for Journaling your Spiritual Journey
Spiritual Writing: Be the Author of Your Own Story
Stop Whining, Choose Life.

# The Sacred Feminine

### James Galluzzo

Gray Wings Press, LLC
Milwaukie, Oregon
2013

# The Sacred Feminine

## By James Galluzzo

Library of Congress Control Number: 2013939085

Requests should be forwarded to diversityasgift@comcast.net

or sent to Gray Wings Press, P.O. Box 593, Clackamas, OR 97015

ISBN 978-0615810690

*Dedicated to the sacred women*
*Who have guided me on the journey*

# The Sacred Feminine

## Six Paintings

The Sacred Feminine is lost and shall be regained. The world as power and control overtakes it, exiling the Bride. Yet when we reconnect to our heart and soul, the Sacred Feminine is embraced. And when the Sacred Feminine is united with the Sacred Masculine, we rediscover our whole self. All people today need this individual reconnection and wholeness. Only then will we move toward peace and holiness, a world of connectedness and Oneness.

By James Galluzzo

# *"Feminine is our guide."*
## *Goethe*

# INTRODUCTION

This book explains my six Sacred Feminine paintings. My inspiration began with my studies on the subject in the early 1960s. I created the paintings in 2012. I used watercolor, egg tempera, ink and markers on heavy watercolor paper. Then I added my own calligraphy on top of the artwork. These paintings are a creative way to help embrace our Sacred Feminine. They are a visual example of key images of the Sacred Feminine to help expand our worldview.

Each chapter discusses one painting and the words on that painting, followed by a set of prayers and hymns that speak to the painting and an explanation of what the painting represents.

# A BRIEF HISTORY OF
# THE SACRED FEMININE

The sacred image is what connected us to life. Humans began to understand this as they grew in wisdom and knowledge. From about 25,000 B.C., the image of the Sacred Feminine was the Great Mother. She was worshipped as the womb, she who gave birth to everything, the great womb which brought forth life. The Great Mother, in her earliest depictions 22,000 years ago, is represented by the goddess figures carved in rock and stone. They encompassed images of the sky, the earth and the cosmos. She was seen in the moon, the sun, the stars, the plants, the trees, the animals and all human beings. The experience was birth and new life. The Sacred Feminine included many roles: goddess, leader, healer, nurturer, Mother of all, the earth and universe.

The Sacred Feminine as Great Mother was the foundation of later cultures all over the world. She was the Tree of Life grounded in our consciousness, which became the life we know as humans, and her fruit became the possibilities for humanity. Her image represents two modes of her divine reality, body and creation, reflecting the creative life that a mother offers her child and with which she nurtures her child.

The voice of the Sacred Feminine came alive with the stories and songs of the goddesses of Sumer and Egypt, and in their temples. The lyrics and prayers to the goddesses were preserved in Egyptian, Canaanite and the gnostic texts. The goddesses adorned the process of life: nurturing, compassion, nature, love, kindness and tenderness. There was harmony throughout this period.

Around 1200 B.C., at the time of patriarchal religion, the Sacred Feminine began to diminish. The Sacred Feminine struggled to hold out wisdom, truth, compassion, beauty and justice in the Roman and Greek goddess images. The image of mother earth, Inanna and Shekinah, as the Hebrew image, helped to keep it alive. However, separation happened when there was a shift of focus between spirit and nature. The male god image gradually became the mind, the protector, the one in charge, the one with power, while the goddess image came to represent nature, the body, feelings, darkness, chaos and evil.

In summary, there were three phases of Sacred Feminine's history:

1. Harmony. The first phase was Harmony. In it the Sacred Feminine was kept alive in images of the Great Mother's body and of creation. These images represent two modes of her divine reality.

2. Role of Sacred Feminine. The Sacred Feminine included many roles: goddess, leader, healer, nurturer, mother of the earth and universe.

3. Dualism creates separation. The third phase of the Sacred Feminine was one of separation. There was a shift of focus from the goddess to the god-above or *power-over* model. It was a radical split between spirit and nature. This shift and split divided the oneness of life into a dualistic way of thinking and living.

The loss of the Sacred Feminine endangered civilization by causing major shifts in how the world functioned. The demise of the Sacred Feminine was reflected in the growth of the power-over concept, as well as humanity's persistent drive for power over nature. All of this created isolation leading to a need to dominate one another, the earth, the nations and the whole world.

This is one of the reasons that the image of the Sacred Feminine is longing to return now. We need to recover our lost relationship with the Sacred Feminine and to find again the true image of the Sacred Masculine.

# WHY IS THE IMAGE OF THE SACRED FEMININE, THE DIVINE MOTHER, SO IMPORTANT?

The answer is the child. Without the consistent and loving care of the feminine, a child gets conditioned away and loses touch with his or her sacredness, goodness, wholeness and holiness. Without nurturing, caring and love, the child begins to believe that he is the conditioned role and no longer the human being filled with potential to grow fully into wisdom and knowledge. Without the wholeness, without the Sacred Masculine and Sacred Feminine being connected, both balancing the other, the child lives in anxiety and fear. The child then ends up choosing to live her role as a victim, unworthy, needy or as an oppressor who bullies and uses *power-over* to perpetuate fear and anxiety. Without the positive image of the feminine, the soul and the body remain separate. In separation and isolation, fear is fueled which leads to power over and control over life. It is like a building with no foundation, easily destroyed by a storm. It is broken and damaged.

We hunger for the return of a model of power-with, where the soul, body, heart and mind work together to restore connectedness, wholeness, abundance and new life.

With the love of the Sacred Feminine and trust in her presence, the child can grow in wisdom and knowledge, in confidence and joy of being himself or herself in life. And it must be recognized that the Sacred Masculine plays a central and important part in this growth. Together, the Sacred Masculine and Sacred Feminine reestablish trust, and together they become teacher, guide, model and light for a new way of living.

# CHAPTER ONE:

## *Her Names*

## Her Names

*(as seen on painting)*

The Great Mother

Divine Feminine

Fire

Red in Color

Sophia

The Bestower of Wisdom

The Girl Child

The Woman

One with Pride

The Eternal One

The Truth

Holy One

She Who Is

One who is Real

Mind

Mother

Full of Knowledge

One Who is Present Everywhere

The Invincible

The Thinking Mind

Mother Goddess

Beautiful

One Who is Loved by All

Adorned by Jewels

One Who Provides Joy

Form of Eternal Bliss

Represents Future

This picture holds the image of the Sacred Feminine that existed in ancient cultures from 5000 to 3500 B.C. before religion came into existence.

The prehistory of the Sacred Feminine is filled with controversy. The main controversy was the issue of one goddess or more, a choice between monotheism or of several images of the Sacred Feminine. The many archetypal images of the Sacred Feminine are in this picture. There was a rich display of divinities and treasures among many ancient cultures. The Sacred Feminine or female spirit represented the earth as the giver of life. Also, there were many images of the fertility goddess, as well as a woman, a star, a tree and a fountain pouring out maternal and sensual qualities.

It is important to go back and look at the Sacred Feminine before institutions, religions and governments discounted the role of the feminine in our history.

This painting shares many of the names given to the Sacred Feminine in these ancient times.

her names

her names

one who provides joy

form of eternal bliss

naming the sacred feminine

adorned by jewels

the thinking mind

represents future

Beautiful

Mother Goddess

one who is loved by all

fire

the eternal One

Woman

One with pride

red in color

sophia

the girl child

the bestower of wisdom

the invincible

the Woman

full of

mother

pure

the Truth

holy one

she who is

knowledge

One who is real

one who is present everywhere

james galluzzo

# PRAYERS TO: *Her Names*

## HYMN TO SACRED FEMININE

Oh! Now beautiful!

The Gold is radiant!

The Gold is radiant, shining, radiant!

For you the sky and the stars

Strike the tambourine

The sun and the moon adore you

The gods revere you

And the goddess sings you hymns.

*From Hymmes et Prieres de l'Egypte Ancienne*

## HYMN

Great one, who became Heaven,

Thou hast assumed power

Thou didst stir

Thou hast filled all places

With thy beauty.

The whole earth lies beneath thee.

Thou had taken possession of it,

Thou enclosed the earth

And all things in thy arms

*H. Frankfurt*

# HYMN

Lady of all powers,

In whom light appears,

Radiant one

Beloved of Heaven and Earth,

Tiara-crowned

Priestess of the Highest God,

My Lady, you are the guardian

Of all greatness.

Your hand holds the seven powers:

You have hung them over your fingers,

You have gathered the many powers,

You have clasped them now

Like necklaces onto your breast.

*Enheduanna –*

*oldest recorded author from Mesopotamia*

# CHAPTER TWO:

# Mother of Passion, Fire and Spirit

# Mother of Fire, Passion & Spirit

*(as seen on painting)*

Mother of Compassion

The Tao is a Mother of all Creation

Universal Mother

Water of Wisdom

Queen of Peace

Gaia

Fire, Passion, Spirit

Wisdom is Glorious

Hail Mother

Daughter

Cosmic Mother

Essence of Compassion

The Divine Feminine

Sacred Heart

Wisdom is Glorious

I am the Rose of Sharon

God is an Abbreviation for Goddess

The Lily of the Valleys

A Religion without a Goddess is
Half Way to Atheism

When You Feel you are Being Moved
by the Creative Spirit;

You Are in Fact Being Moved by the
Divine Feminine

The goddess of fire, passion and spirit is a healing image that is a flame so vast it encompasses the stars in the cosmos. The flame can hold the hardness of heat, can balance the shadow and light, can heal old wounds and can bring the male and female into true human connection.

This image is often seen as the Goddess Pele, the goddess of fire and passion who created passion to lead to renewal, rebirth, reform, warmth, love and connection. She stands strong against dualism in any form.

She challenges any conditioning that makes women or men less than human. She fights against oppressors and victims. She calls all people to reconnect to their birth and rekindles the spirit of fire and passion that leads to a oneness with all of creation.

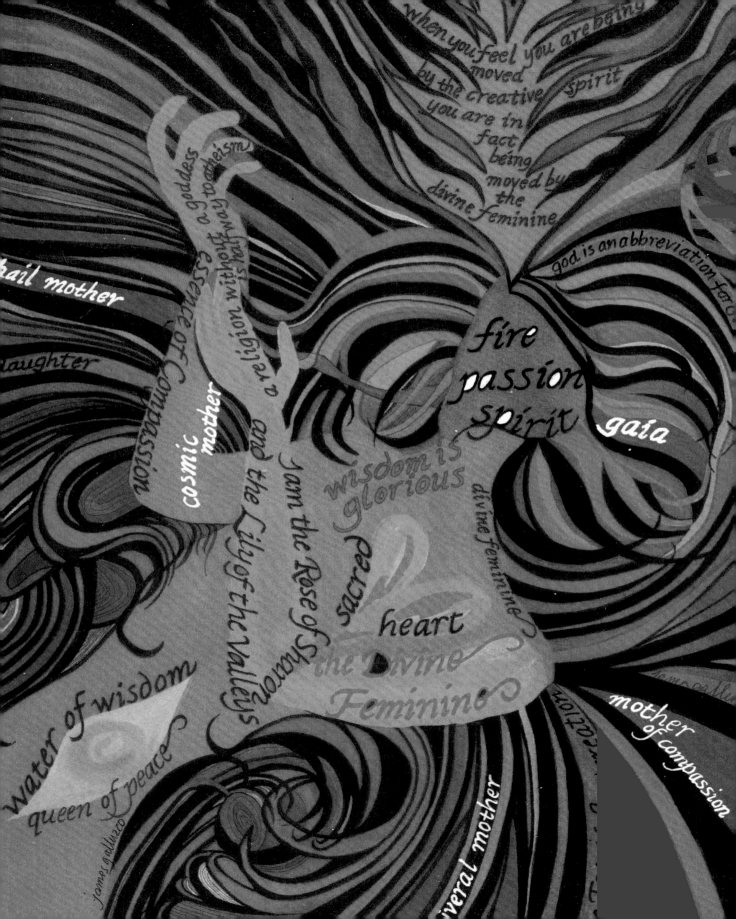

# PRAYERS TO: Mother of Fire, Passion & Spirit

## HYMN TO GAIA

Mother of all
The foundation, the oldest one
I shall sing to Earth
She feeds everything that is in the world
with Passion, Fire and Spirit

## PRAYERS

Hail Mother
Bring a sense of passion to my life
Filled with fire
Making us a living Spirit in the World


Mother of Fire, Passion and Spirit
Bring us back to life.
Help to reconnect to your desire
To live life fully
And to be filled with the
Spirit of Passion
*James Galluzzo*

# I AM THE FIRE OF THE FEMININE RAY

Praise be to the Divine Mother
The Inscrutable power in all things.
Praise be to the Divine Mother
The Intelligence in all beings.
Praise be to the Divine Mother
The Forgiveness in all things.
Praise be to the Divine Mother
The Peacefulness in all things.
Praise be to the divine Mother
The Faithfulness in all things.
Praise be to the Divine Mother
The beauty in all things.

Praise be to the Divine Mother
The Mercy in all things.
Praise be to the divine Mother
The Consciousness in all things.
You are the Mother of the universe
Let your mercy shine on all.
*Devi-mahatmya*

I AM a being, a violet fire!
I AM the purity God desires!

# CHAPTER THREE
## Mother Earth

# Mother Earth
*(as seen on painting)*

She is the Awareness of Our Species

She is the Tree of Life

Holy Blessed Mother Earth

Respect Trees, Life, Water, Plants

Mother Earth

Her Divine Presence Graced the Earth

The Eternal Feminine is Our Guide

The Divine Mother Heals and

Consoles Earth

Mother Earth Kindly Set Me Down

upon a Well Founded Place

Goddess of the Forest

---

Gaia was the goddess that was known as Earth or Mother Earth. She gave birth to the sea and the sky without male intervention. In Greece, Gaia was considered the basis from which all the gods were born. In Rome, she was known as Terra.

The myriad faces of Mother Earth explain her being. She is both a gentle healer and a fearless warrior. She can be tender and delightful or ferocious when necessary. "A small piece was mother, a drop was Krishna, a little was Buddha, and a touch of Christ," says Swami Vivkenanda.

The idea of the Sacred Feminine transcends all religions.

- In Jewish tradition, Shekinah meaning Divine Presence.

- In Hinduism, Shakti.

- In Buddhism, Prajuaparamita.

- In Egyptian tradition, Isis.

- In the Old Testament and Apocrypha, Wisdom.

- In Christian Gnostics, Sophia or Pistis Sophia meaning Faith Wisdom.

- In Christianity, the Madonna or Blessed Mary.

Lex Hixon, an 18th century songwriter described Mother Earth as:

"youthful, ancient, and ageless. She is divine creativity, evolutionary energy, timeless awareness, transcendent reality, and is every woman. She is the feminine principle within male and female persons."

Mother Earth is often depicted as the color green since green is life giving, such as: tree of life, the forest and woods. She both grows life and gives forth life.

goddess of the forest
the eternal feminine is our guide
he is self awareness of our species
Her Divine Presenc
She is the tree of Life
holy
Mother Earth
mother earth, kindly set me down
upon a well
founded place
the Divine Mother heals and consoles Earth
Respect
trees
therEarth
life
water
ir
plants
James galluzzo

# Prayers to: *Mother Earth*

The Divine Mother revealed to me in the

Kali Temple that is was

She who had become everything,

She showed me that everything was full of Consciousness.

The Image was Consciousness,

The altar was Consciousness,

The water-vessels were Consciousness,

The door-still was consciousness,

The marble floor was Consciousness—all was consciousness.

*Ramakrishna*

I am the Queen, source of thought,

Knowledge itself!

You do not know Me, yet

You dwell in Me.

I announce Myself in words both

Gods and humans welcome.

From the summit of the world,

I give birth to the sky!

The tempest is My breath, all living

Creatures are My life!

Beyond, the wide earth,

Beyond the vast heaven,

My grandeur extends forever.

*Devi Sukta*

# CHAPTER FOUR

## Holy Sophia

# Holy Sophia

*(as seen on painting)*

Mother

Sophia

Peace Maker

Sophia, Lady of the Evening

Mother Stretch your Wings

Giver of Life

Sister

Let me be One like the
Imperishable Stars

Saint

Beloved of Heaven and Earth

She is Light Itself and Transcendent
Heart Mother

She is the Lady of Heaven and Earth Having
Brought them into Existence
through What Her Heart Conceived

She is so Pure

She Pervades and Permeates All Things

Priestess

Holy Mother Earth, the Trees and all Nature
are Witness to Your Thoughts & Deeds

Earth Mother

Lover

Radiant One

I Sing

Might Majestic & Radiant Shine Brilliantly

Sophia Speaks

Greatest of Love

Mistress of Women who Fills Heaven and
Earth with Beauty

Holy Sophia is known as the Mother of All. As Wisdom she deeply loved humans and chose to live among them. Humans rejected her, but she offers those who search for wisdom and love an experience of Sophia.

Sophia's traits include wisdom, love, communication, creativity, giving, and trust. Sophia is the truth and tells it as it is. Sophia is the mother of faith, hope and love.

Sophia represents Wisdom, the Wisdom that was given to Solomon. The myth is that Solomon married Sophia and the union created trust, compassion and wisdom.

The presence of Sophia brings hope, life and light, a true holy spirit. Sophia conveys the essence of God. The dove has always been one of the great images of the spirit. Also, the image of the flame represents a joyous flame. Fresh, cool air brings love that flows within the heart.

Sophia brings a whirlwind of creative thought and gives way to imagination.

Sophia holds the sacred heart.

mother

sophia

Sophia, Lady of the evening

Mother, stretch your wings, let me be one like the imperishable stars

earth mother

earth mother

sister

might majestic & radiant shine brilliantly

I Sing

giver of life

radiant one

Cover

sophia speaks

all nature are witness to your thoughts and deeds

priestess

greatest of love
mistress of women
who fills heaven & earth
with Beauty

she is so pure, she pervades &

she is so pure she pervades & permeates all things

James galluzzo

Mother Earth, the trees, &

She is the Lady of Heaven and Earth having brought them into existence through what her heart conceived

heart mother

beloved of heaven and earth

light it self or transcendent

peace maker

she is so pure she pervades & permeates all things

saint

mrs galluzzo

# Prayers to: *Holy Sophia*

## SOPHIA

You of the whirling wings,

circling, encompassing energy of God:

you quicken the world in your clasp.

One wing soars in heaven,

one wing sweeps the earth,

and the third flies all around us.

Praise to Sophia!

Let all the earth praise her!

*Hildegard of Bingen*


In the space within the heart are contained

both heaven and earth.

*Upanishads*

# THE HAIL SOPHIA

Hail Sophia, filled with Light, the Christ is with thee.

Blessed art thou among all human beings

and blessed is the liberator of thy Light, Jesus.

Holy Sophia, Mother of all Gods,

pray to the Light for us thy children,

now & in the hour of our death.

Hail, Lady of Light

Mystical Lover of my spirit.

Blessed are you, Woman of Wisdom,

and blessed are the gifts you bestow on us your children.

Holy Sophia, goddess who leads to the One God,

fill me with your emptiness,

and darken my spirit with your light. AMEN

CHAPTER FIVE

# Madonna

# Madonna

*(as seen on painting)*

Hail Mary

Lady of the Angels

Queen of Heaven

Blessed Among Women

Gentle Woman

Power With

Hail Holy Queen

Hail Our Life

Our Sweetness

Our Hope

Queen of Peace

Prima Materia

Love

Life

Tears

Mercy

Hope

Sweetness

Wisdom

Grace

Sacred Heart

Virgin

Mother

Mary in the Christian tradition carries forth four thousand years of goddess images. She is called the queen of heaven as was Inanna, Ishtar and Isis. She is seen as the mother of earth, the morning star as well as the moon, whose crescent is often her pedestal. Like other goddesses, Mary became the Queen of the Sea. Like Aphrodite and Kuan Yin, Mary became the mother, the Holy Mother.

Mary stands as the intercessor between heaven and earth. She is the image of compassion and healing. She held her son when he was a baby and when he was taken off the cross.

Mary's name comes from the Latin word mare, the sea. Mary takes on the image that Shekinah held. Mary became the Prima Materia, the Womb of Creation.

In scripture, Mary is humble and quiet, but within a few hundred years, she takes on the history of the great goddesses before her. She became both the Virgin and the Mother of God.

As the Madonna, she is seen as the Mother of all life.

# PRAYERS TO: *Madonna*

Hail, Holy Queen, Mother of Mercy

Hail our life, our sweetness and our hope.

To thee do we cry, poor banished children of Eve,

To thee do we send up our signs, mourning and weeping

In this vale of tears.

Turn then, most glorious advocate,

Thine eyes of mercy toward us

And after this our exile, show unto us

The blessed Fruit of thy womb

O merciful, O loving, O sweet Virgin Mary

I am the Queen of Peace

Mary is the real woman who lived

Her life from her heart

She is the symbol and archetype of the heart itself,

There is Something Infinite in Being Mother of the Infinite.

*Thomas of Villanova*

My soul proclaims your greatness

and my spirit rejoices in You

for You have looked with favor upon your servant

and from this day forward

all generations will call me blessed.

     *Luke 1: 46-49*


For the Blessed Virgin, who was to be His Mother, God created the
entire universe.

     *St. Bernard of Clairvaux*


Mother of Divine Love.

She invites us to live from our hearts.

     *The Virgin Mary Speaking at Medjugori June 24, 1981*


Mary is everywhere

The true tree that bears the fruit of life,

And the real mother that produces it.

     *Louis-Marie Grignion de Monfort*

# CHAPTER 6
## Cosmic Mother

# Cosmic Mother

*(as seen on painting)*

Cosmic Mother

Lover of the Cosmic Dance

Mother Nature

She Grounds all People

Holy Mother Earth

Nature is a Witness to your Deeds

Goddess of all Creation

Holder of the Moon

The Cosmic Mother pictures the Sacred Feminine as relating to the cosmos, the extraterrestrial vastness of the universe, including the earth.

The Cosmic Mother is concerned with spiritual, theological, mystical, philosophical and psychological ideas characterized by greatness, especially in extent, intensity, or comprehensiveness.

The Cosmic Mother holds the planets, the stars, the moon, the sun, the mountains, the river, the plants, the trees, the animals, the birds, the fish; and she lays the foundation, the first Chakra, for all people.

# PRAYERS TO: *Cosmic Mother*

I say, "Hail" to the Holy One who appears in the heaven!

I say, "Hail" to the Holy Priestess of heaven.

I say "Hail" to First Daughter of the moon!

Mighty, majestic and radiant,

You shine brilliantly in the evening,

You brighten the day at dawn,

You stand in the heavens like the sun and the moon,

Your wonders are known both above and below,

To the greatness of the Holy Priestess in heaven,

To you, I sing.

*From Inanna, Queen of Heaven and Earth*


The Holy One stands all alone,

In the clear sky

Upon all the lands and upon

The black-haired people,

The people as numerous as sheep,

The Lady looks in sweet wonder

From heaven's midst;

They parade before the Holy One

The Lady of the evening,

She is lofty

The Maid, I would praise as is fitting.

The Lady of the evening is lofty

On the horizon.

*The Poetry of Sumer*

Mighty, majestic and radiant,

You shine brilliantly in the evening,

You brighten the day at dawn.

You stand in the heavens like the sun and the moon,

Your wonders are known both above and below,

To the greatness of the holy priestess in heaven.

*Queen of Heaven and Earth*


## LADY OF THE LARGEST HEART

She goes out

White-sparked, radiant

In the dark vault of evening's sky

Star-steps in the street

Through the Gate of Wonder

*Enheduanna, Lady of the Largest Heart*

This book emerges from the need for a coming together of the Sacred Feminine and the Sacred Masculine. The time is now to embrace the Sacred Feminine, but not to the demise of the Sacred Masculine; the time is now to recover a sense of trust and cooperation, peace and justice, hope and joy in life.

We see the need for relationships and the need for wholeness, for a oneness. With wholeness and oneness we can then embrace the inherent human qualities that are true for every human being, male and female, and see the Sacred Feminine and the Sacred Masculine in every single person.

The Sacred Masculine will be the subject of the next series. The third series will embrace the Sacred Masculine and the Sacred Feminine as one.

*"God is our father; even more, God is our mother."*

*Pope John Paul I*

# JAMES GALLUZO

*JAMES GALLUZZO has been a spiritual director and guide for 25 years, working with individuals, teaching classes, and giving retreats. He is an artist, author, priest, teacher, administrator, diversity trainer, and spiritual director.*

*Fr. Galluzzo is the author of: A Spiritual Handbook: A Resource for Travelers and Guides on the Journey, The Spirituality of Mary Magdalene, Jesus as Liberator and the Gospel Values, Quotes and Reflection Questions for Journaling your Spiritual Journey, Spiritual Writing: Be the Author of Your Own Story, and Stop Whining, Choose Life.*

*He founded Allies: People to People, an organization that teaches a way of living and thinking that honors human liberation based on the Gospel values, and that works to end oppression of any kind: sexism, racism, classism, ageism, adultism, and homophobia.*

*Fr. Galluzzo is the director of the non-profit organization Diversity as Gift that works to honor all and teach about dignity from a spiritual perspective. He is also the director of the Urban Spirituality Center in Portland, Oregon.*

*He holds a BA degree from Gonzaga University, an MAT degree from Reed College, an Administrative Certificate from Lewis and Clark College, an MA degree in Theology from Catholic University of America, Mount Angel Seminary, and Portland State University.*

*Fr. Galluzzo leads workshops throughout the country on Conflict Resolution, Community Building, Diversity, Gospel Values, Spirituality, and Human Liberation.*

Acknowledgements

In gratitude for help and guidance from

Susan Hammond
Annie Doyle
Mary Gonzales
Sheree Tuppan
Jan Kruger for envisioning the cover concept

Book and Cover Design by Karen Gatens, Gatens Design